The

B

SP

Debbie Barham

Text by Debbie Barham

Summersdale Publishers Ltd
46 West Street
Chichester
West Sussex
PO19 1RP
UK

www.summersdale.com

Printed and bound in Denmark by Nørhaven Paperback.

ISBN 1 84024 288 4

INTRODUCTION

'Beware the man of one book' – *St Thomas Aquinas*

'Reading maketh a full man' – *Sir Francis Bacon*

'Reading maketh a particularly dreary holiday destination' –
Berkshire Tourist Board

Building up your own personal library over the years can be an intensely rewarding and mind-expanding experience, broadening your intellectual horizons, and leaving you with a valuable literary legacy to bequeath to your grateful descendants.

But let's face it: that takes absolutely bloody *ages*. And you've got far better things to do than hang about in dusty second-hand bookshops getting lecherous glances from that dodgy bloke in the cagoule fingering a Longfellow in the Poetry section, or winking at you from behind a Trollope. Your grateful descendants will probably just bequeath all your first editions to a car boot sale anyway, and all those ugly books simply *ruin* your fashionably minimalist Scandinavian-style shelving (not to mention collecting loads of dust). What's a would-be literary aficionado to do? It's a modern dilemma that even the Domestic Goddess doesn't have an answer for.

Now, at last, there's a solution: *The Little Book of Books*. Together for the first time in one handy, pocket-sized volume is everything you need to know about the must-have tomes of recent years, condensed, abridged, and guaranteed to go 33 per cent further than your ordinary Big Books formula.

Become instantly well-read overnight! Never again fear the social suicide of (Aaaargh! Cripes! Bugger!) never having read *Bridget Jones's Diary,* being too stressed-out to buy *The Little Book of Calm,* or remaining better acquainted with Captain Birds Eye's cod fingers than *Captain Corelli's Mandolin.*

No longer need you confuse your Harry Potter with your Harold Pinter, your Delia Smith with your Zadie Smith or your Simon Schama with your Karma Sutra (which could have disastrous effects on your love life: there's nothing more off-putting to a prospective partner than a condom dated 'Best Before 1603 BC').

Thanks to *The Little Book of Books* you never need buy another tiresome, unsightly book again in your entire life.★

So chuck out your Chicklits, ditch your Dickens and consign the rest of your library to the nearest litter(ature) bin. Pop *The Little Book of Books* inside your handbag, and you'll be well-ready for anything!

★ Except, obviously, *The Second Little Book of Books*.

FICTION

Man and Wrist

Bestselling newspaper journalist Tony Parsimonious completes his trilogy of deeply moving contemporary novels with this final work in which a bestselling newspaper journalist finally gets to grips with his confused personal life by rediscovering the one true love of his teenage years – his own right hand.

The Perm

John Grisham's latest mystery is set in the cut-throat, backstabbing world of modern hairdressing in San Francisco. A careless blow-dry turns into a frantic game of cut-and-mousse – in which more than one person will have to dye …

The Nice Man Cometh

Hugely powerful but ultimately anticlimactic American-Irish drama in which a wayward, henpecked husband considers blowing his ceaselessly nagging wife's brains out with a high-powered assault rifle. But then decides not to, after all . . .

Shite Teeth

Martin Amos' thinly disguised autobiographical account of growing up in London literary society and being regarded as an outcast because of his substandard dental health is a critically acclaimed masterpiece. Defying all the odds, foul-mouthed Amos becomes successful, obnoxious and vain enough to fork out a six-figure sum and have his gnashers cosmetically fixed. Truly heartwarming.

The Life of Po

Bizarre, genre-defying Booker nominee, centred around the oceanic wanderings of a young boy who finds himself cast adrift in the Pacific with a giant red Teletubby touting a plastic handbag for company. As they abandon themselves to the whims of the tempestuous sea, our hero is forced to pass the time by debating with his acrylic-covered companion the mysteries of life, love, religion, the futility of existence and the best recipe for Tubby Custard. A task only slightly hampered by the fact that Po can pronounce just three regonisable words: '*Eh*', '*Oh*', and '*Eh-Oh*'.

Dad and Lad by Guy Mann

Beer-swilling, Gunners-supporting 'New Lad' finds his whole perspective on life completely unaltered by fatherhood, because he never comes back from the pub in case the squalling, repellent little brat needs its nappy changing or something. And it probably isn't even his.

Mars Bar

The long-awaited sequel to the bestselling *Chocolat*, in which the heroine embarks on more erotic adventures after a chance meeting with Marianne Faithfull.

Captain Corelli's MP3 Player

A suave Italian soldier arrives to head the invading troops on a remote island, whose simple, homely people are slowly won over by his charmingly playing them bootlegged versions of Britney Spears 'Ooops, I Did It Again' and S Club 7's 'Don't Stop Moving', on his top-of-the-range PDA device.

The Placid House

Irwin Scott, the former *enfant terrible* of Scottish literature, mellows slightly in his advanced years, with this compilation of short stories about a group of senior citizens who spend their time taking Mogadon, listening to Perry Como LPs, and committing petty pension-book fraud in order to finance their increasing dependence on bags of white, crystalline, denture-cleaning powder. Includes the notorious 'shat maeself in mae own bed' scene.

Fatal Flutter by Francis Dicks

Multi-million-selling thriller writer abandons the Sport of Kings for this latest fast-moving crimefest, this time set in the high-octane field of professional pigeon racing. Can the 'lofty' ambitions of Ron Mottershead, Barnsley's arrogant young newcomer to the Fancy, depose the reigning champion – and when Ron's favourite cock is found stiff and cold one morning, who's been spreading poisoned seed? Thrill and Trill go hand in hand in a gripping tale to keep both blokes and birds on the edge of their perch.

Cold Comfort Form

A delicious satire on modern bureaucracy, telling the story of practical, down-to-earth young Flora who goes to live with a family of simple farming folk and becomes embroiled in the hilariously absurd requirements of EC Livestock And Agricultural Subsidy Subcommittee paperwork, all of which needs to be filled out in triplicate in order to receive a £1.50 grant for growing non-existent apple trees.

Three Men On A Cruise

A charming whimsy in which a trio of bachelors take an eventful late-night dip in Highgate Men's Bathing Pool. Packed with rollicking good laughs, such as the episodes where Harris attempts to open a condom packet in the dark without the aid of a tin-opener, George recalls his frustrations at putting up a poster of Kylie Minogue, and Montmorency gets off with a former Secretary of State for Trade and Industry in a two-man ridge tent.

Also recommended: *Three Men in a Botox Clinic*, the follow-up volume in which the same trio of bachelors suffer a simultaneous mid-life crisis and become obsessively vain about their physical appearance. They fancifully invest a small fortune in AHA-enriched moisturisers and BriteSmile tooth-whitening treatments, and demand thrice-weekly injections at the Harley Street Male

Enhancement Unit to improve their muscle definition beneath their tight Lycra T-shirts. However, they still bemoan the fact that the only sex they're getting is when the dog chooses to hump their leg under the camping table.

CHILDREN'S LITERATURE

The Big Friendly Gnat

Roald Dahl's cautionary fable about a lovable yet misunderstood blood-sucking insect, cruelly shunned by local children because of his tendency to plunge a long, slender proboscis into their juicy flesh and gorge himself on their warm, sticky fluids, before departing to hatch out a seething mass of maggot-like larvae in the nearest fresh dog turd. In this enchantingly illustrated tale, the BFG learns to gain human acceptance by generously using his horny nasal mandible to perform free body-piercings and tattoos for rebellious teenage dropouts – and realises the true quality of friendship, before being fatally twatted with a rolled up copy of the *Daily Star*.

Five Have A Wonderful Ad Venture

The continuing escapades of Enid Blyton's young heroes, now occupying a trendy warehouse-style loft apartment in London's fashionable Soho and running successful advertising agency BBJDAGH Ltd (Bartle, Bogle, Julian, Dick, Anne, George and Hegarty the dog). In this, the first of ten new stories, Julian shoves lashings of simply *wizard* Columbian coke up his nose, George secures a jolly spiffing account to promote ginger beer on the Alcopops market, whilst Dick spots a pair of scoundrels smuggling contraband into the country – and manages to negotiate a bulk discount on several kilos of finest Grade A narcotics.

Meg and Morgue

The much-loved *Meg and Mog* series grows increasingly dark and gothic. After the tragic passing away of elderly pussycat Mog in *Goodbye Mog*, Meg visits the Pet Cemetery and (with echoes of Stephen King) is found the following morning – her heart ripped out, her horrifically mutilated corpse raked by the deep clawmarks of some monstrous, cat-like beast from Beyond The Grave, and a giant cat turd deposited at her feet in an eerily chilling territorial warning. One for older children.

Three Lions, The Pitch and the Wardrobe

Fantastical tale of how a group of young lads venture into a wardrobe full of clothes, and stumble upon an amazing, mystical realm where you can be paid a million pounds for wearing trendy sports gear, or don pink nail varnish and a sarong and still be hailed as a national hero by blokes in pubs.

The *Mister Men* Series

Laugh and learn with the hilarious antics of Mr Bump, Mr Naughty, Mr Busy, Mr Tickle, Mr Small and all their little friends. Now incorporating colourful new characters, specially designed to introduce younger readers to the harsh realities of modern-day Britain: Mr Tipple (the alcoholic), Mr Stump (the angst-ridden pubescent with the embarrassing public erection problem), Mr Nosy (the glue-sniffer), Mr Snorty (the coke addict), Mr Buzzy (the 'E' abuser) and Little Miss Bump (the Teenage Mother, currently engaged in a paternity suit with Mr Bing, the Hollywood Film Mogul).

AUTOBIOGRAPHY

My Lefty Foot

The touchingly poignant autobiography of former socialist firebrand Michael Foot, and his heartbreakingly futile attempts to make himself heard when the weight of his mouldering donkey jacket prevented him from physically moving any limb above his own waist.

The Big C

A moving, sometimes shocking account of the author's struggle to come to terms with discovering he had 'The Big C'… Dyslexia. How, as an inspiration to fellow sufferers, he offered to write a weekly column about his complaint for a national newspaper, but was rejected on the basis that with his literacy skills he would only ever get a job subbing on *The Guardian*. A truly tear-jerking book, bravely written without the aid of an auto Spell-Checker.

Wild Svens

Seen through the eyes of one spirited young woman, this Oriental epic tells the story of early twenty-first century Japan and Korea during the turbulent period of the World Cup – an unforgettable tale of tyranny, hope, and ultimate heartbreak as heroine Ulrika tries to continue her doomed relationship with powerful overlord Sven Goran Eriksson in the face of relentless persecution.

Skinner

Popular stand-up comedian and left-wing radical Dennis Skinner's often outrageous memoirs. 'Gross … highly offensive … not even remotely funny' *Daily Lame*.

A Prison Diary by FF8283

An extremely distressing and unnerving account of British prison life, by the unfortunate individual who was punished for a litany of grisly crimes by being forced to share a cell with prisoner number FF8282 (Archer). The felon consequently witnessed, at first hand, the disgraced peer's brutal butchery of the English language whilst hacking out yet another new novel. Not for the faint-hearted.

BIOGRAPHY

Life of Apes

David Attenborough, TV's most respected naturalist (and author of *Life of Mammals* and *Life of Birds*), spent several months observing the almost human habits of these hairy-knuckled, stomach-thumping primates in their native environment in order to produce possibly the most insightful and authoritative biography of the Gallagher brothers yet to be written. (Attenborough is now working on volume two of his Oasis retrospective, provisionally entitled *Life of Beatles*).

SPORT

Australia's Ashes

The relentlessly miserable memoir of an English Test Cricket team who leave their homeland in search of better prospects Down Under, but find the Lucky Country equally grim when they lose four matches on the hop in a tragic, degrading and unremittingly bleak fashion. A depressing read.

A Brief History of Extra Time

Sir Alex Ferguson expounds his personal theories about Quantum Mechanics, in which the time-space continuum can be scientifically warped when you decide you need the ref to blow up a few minutes early, or need another season or two before you retire.

The Making of '007'
Exclusive, behind-the-scenes look at the international phenomenon which is an average English Test Cricket innings.

Rivaldo Down!

Heroic action on the battlefields of the Far East, when one man's bravery in acting as though he has just been shot in the head (and subsequently falling over in the penalty box) saves his country from certain defeat against Turkey in the World Cup group stages and inspires them to a historic victory in the Final.

Vinny Jones' Diary

'Monday. Units of alcohol: 30 (v. good). Psychiatric units: 2. Pounds gained (in Hollywood film deals): 5 million. Crikey!'

The angst-ridden chronicle of neurotic young media professional, Vinny, and his tumultuous personal life, most of which revolves around getting drunk, failing to meet any nice men, and hanging out with his great mates Guy and Mazza.

From Russia With Six-Love

Anna Kournikova reveals the secrets of how a complete inability to actually play tennis has failed to hinder her from becoming the world's highest-paid female tennis player.

TRAVEL

The Good Tramp Site Guide

Wino Jake and his dog Dog review the best of Britain's doss-spots, shop doorways, park benches, bus shelters and railway waiting-rooms, noting such amenities as hot and cold running urine, quality of food in local dustbins, and proliferation of entertainment facilities (e.g., road accident blackspot, branch of Radio Rentals with window display sets not tuned to Channel 5).

The Ken-Tucki Expedition

Tale of an extraordinary journey whereby five explorers endeavour, against all the odds, to cross the United States of America surviving solely on Family Buckets of fried chicken with a crispy barbecue-style coating. But, tragically, they die of cholesterol poisoning before they make it.

A Year In Preston

A family of French wine-growers escape their rustic chateau in the sleepy Loire valley to start a new life abroad: scrounging dole on a Northern England council estate, experiencing the *joie de vivre* of inner-city race riots and having abuse shouted at them in the street on a daily basis by the quaint, colourful locals.

Round Iceland With A Fridge

Hastily churned-out response to Tony Hawks' publishers demanding a successor to his unexpected bestseller *Round Ireland With A Fridge*. In this second volume of travelogues, the author takes his trusty Zanussi to his local deep-freeze grocery emporium and stocks up on fish fingers, oven chips, family-sized bags of peas and tubs of Chunky Monkey Häagen-Dasz without the need to invest in a cool-bag.

Pole to Pole

Michael Palin's marathon attempt to obtain a lap-dance in every poledancing club from Land's End to John O'Groats.

On The Ring Road

Jack Kerouac for the commuter generation. The drugs (Pro-Plus, travel sickness pastilles), the music (Chris de bloody Burgh on Heart 106.2 FM on the car stereo), the speed (5 mph average), the drink (Blue Boar Max-PaxTM coffee), and the open road (Closed Until Further Notice. We Apologise For The Inconvenience) from the viewpoint of a stressed-out middle manager cruisin' in his BMW 320i on the M25.

HISTORY

A History of Britain – 17:59 – 20:02

Simon Schama tackles the sole period of British history not yet chronicled in his bestselling series of works, with this enlightening look back at the extraordinary happenings that took place between 6 p.m. and 8 p.m. last Wednesday evening.

PHOTOGRAPHY

Stretchmarks

Post-natal sequel to the controversial *Sex* by Madonna, featuring lavishly-mounted, moodily-lit, titillating shots of the chart-topping singer restrained by stirrups, having her nipples sucked, and lounging seductively beside a birthing pool. And somewhat less titillating shots of her standing at the sink, trying to scrub the amalgamated residue of dribble, sick and congealed breastmilk out of her favourite metallic bra.

PERSONAL DEVELOPMENT

Learning To Love Your Self

Personal development manual for those who find it hard to comprehend the popularity of Will Self's shamelessly onanistic literary efforts. Written by William Self, with a Foreword by W. Self.

TECHNOLOGY

How To Design Really Irritating Websites!
</BLINK>

A step-by-step guide to creating stunning, professional-looking Internet sites that get right on people's tits. There are 500 full-colour pages with far too many pictures, only 15 of which actually contain any information that you actually want to know. Several sentences are inexplicably picked out in HUGE FLASHING CAPITAL LETTERS with no index. Also available in an Intensely Aggravating Pop-Up edition. Book only viewable with MicroSoft Contact Lenses v7.0. Page 404 not found: please return to your bookstore or try again later.

Computers For Brummies

The complex world of technology is made simple for people from the Black Country in this helpful book. Never again be bamboozled by tricky jargon. This book simplifies it into phrases every West Midlands-dweller can understand, including *Error: Do You Want To Quit Y/N?* ('Yow gan an dun summink styowpid! Yow wanna gan awa' or wot: Aaar/Naar?'), *Operating System* ('Fackin' bastaad Moycrosaft Windaas') and *Internet* ('Wor Aston Villa nie ganna put the feckin' ball').

TV TIE-INS

Have I Got News For You –
The Scripts

Written by Angus Deayton's fifteen off-the-cuff gag writers. Side-splitting compilation of spontaneous witty retorts delivered by TV's Mr Sex Scandal from way back in that Golden Era of British Comedy (circa 2001) when the only funny lines Mr Deayton was associated with were those on the autocue.

EDUCATIONAL

Lette's Study Guides

Great works of literature from the current GCSE syllabus, condensed by bestselling antipodean authoress Kathy Lette into slim volumes of pun-laden feminist chick-lit with gaudy covers.

PARENTING

Zen and the Art of Child Maintenance

A seminal work in which the author embarks on an epic cross-country journey to escape extortionate monthly CSA bills, during which he wrestles with some of life's eternal philosophical quandaries, applying ancient Chinese thinking to such modern dilemmas as *Are You Sure He's My Son?*, *You Want HOW MUCH per Month???* and *Oh Boy! Why The Hell Didn't I Use A Condom?*

The Lillet Book of Calm

The perfect solution for cack-handed modern parents, unsure of how to broach the delicate subject of menstruation with their prepubescent female offspring. Also suitable for women with particularly unenlightened boyfriends who suffer an acute panic attack if tasked with the job of 'popping into Boots and picking up a packet of tampons on your way home'.

RELIGION

The Saint Nick Verses

For readers of 5 and upwards. Salman Rushdie's notoriously blasphemous attempt to incur the wrath of parents worldwide, debunking the myth about the existence of a so-called 'Santa Claus' figure once and for all.

FASHION AND LIFESTYLE

What Not To Wear, Vol. II

Glossy and lavishly-illustrated hardback version of the Spring/Summer 2003 Great Universal Home Shopping Catalogue.

I Can't Believe It's Not Clutter!

Britain's leading Clutter Therapist (and host of BBC2's *Stop F★★★ing Your Life Up And Throw Away Those 5,000 Smelly Old Tesco Bags From Under Your Sink, You Pathetic Individual* programme) explains how an ordered home begets an ordered mind, and reveals how day-to-day financial woes can be miraculously banished simply by reorganising your front room so as not to clutter your coffee table with so many large and extortionately overpriced coffee-table books, such as this one.

ETIQUETTE

Debrett's Guide to the 21st Century

Post-millennial manners explained. Does society deem it ladylike to have TXT on a first date? Is it expected for you to arrive 'fashionably late' for an appointment? (Answer: Only if you're driving a Connex Southeast train). How should you address a member of the Royal Family when he has just referred to your entire race as 'slitty-eyed Chinkies', 'smelly Dagos' or 'work-shy Wop b★★★★★ds'? And when meeting a disgraced former President of the USA, does decorum dictate that you bow your head and drop down on one knee, or will this just give Bill the wrong idea?

COOKERY

Oliver's Kitchen

Fifty-six historically accurate recipes from the Victorian workhouse, as popularised in the novels of Charles Dickens. Surprise your dinner party guests (*Arrive 18:00. Drinks 18:15. Dinner 1838*) with such trendily retro-chic dishes as cold gruel, hot gruel, tepid gruel, no gruel, and (for those who prefer their Victoriana with a modern Twist) gruel artfully drizzled with a piquant confit of cranberry and crème fraîche. *Oat cuisine* at its finest, with presentation tips including how to infect your guests with rickets and syphilis, and suggested utensils for beating them black and blue if they dare solicit a second helping. Very more-ish.

Edwina Bites

The former Tory turned bestselling author compiles a collection of her favourite egg recipes, including Smoked Salmonella and several dishes best served cold (e.g., Hard-Boiled Revenge). Also features some lethal curries guaranteed to keep you on the John all night, and keep returning up to fourteen years later.

Geri's Kitchen

Compiled by the former personal nutritionist of Ms Halliwell, the 'Main Courses' section of this new low-fat cookbook has over 101 brand new recipes for a skinless, organically-reared chicken breast fillet and half a lettuce leaf. The 'Dessert' section includes creative suggestions for luxury ice cream, Tennessee Toffee Pie, chocolate fudge cake, Mars bars, sponge pudding and custard, fresh cream eclairs, doughnuts, Mr Kipling individual Bakewell tarts, pecan pie and your own index finger rammed down the back of your oesophagus. *'Puke-a!'*

THRILLERS

Clear and Present Donger
by Tom Chancy

The continuing, tension-packed exploits of CIA inspector Jack Ryan, who finds that the feeling of macho superiority which holding a large, sleek, death-dealing firearm engenders in him has given him a permanent erection in his military-issue trousers. Ryan faces his toughest challenge yet – evading arrest by the LAPD for public indecency and convincing sceptical investigators that it really is just a gun in his pocket.

ART

Post-Modern Pat

More enchanting tales of the Greendale delivery man who bolsters his pathetic Consignia salary with a lucrative sideline in conceptualist art installations inspired by *enfant terrible* Damien Hirst. In this first book, Pat courageously delivers Mrs Miggins' Christmas presents through a snowdrift, then goes home to chloroform his black-and-white cat, slice it in half with a butcher's cleaver and pickle it in a tankful of formaldehyde.

PHILOSOPHY

Stupid Kant!

Latest in the blockbuster series of great philosophical works simplified for the school-age market. From the author of *When We Were Very Jung*, *The Joy of Socrates*, and *You Know Foucault About Anything*.

Aristotle and the Philosopher's Stone

Well-meaning but futile attempt by publishers to engage young minds in the works of the Great Greek Thinker by rebinding his collected tracts in a bright red paperback with a cartoon of a geeky boy and an owl on the front in the hope that they might think it is a new J. K. Rowling.

POLITICS

Are You Teresa Gorman?

Adapted from a successful stand-up act at the Westminster playhouse, the former Conservative Member for Billericay, Teresa Gorman, relates her experiences travelling round the country trying to track down the handful of people who share her radically right-wing views. Packed with shaggy-dog Tories and colourful comedy characters, this book will delight anyone who enjoyed previous bestseller *Alan Clarke – Ha Ha Ha*.

Currieolanus

Shakespearean tragedy of backstabbing, treachery, and a doomed relationship between a future leader – Iannus Majoris – and his lowly servant-girl, Edwina Salmonella, set in the dim and distant era of the last Conservative administration.

HEALTH AND BEAUTY

The Hypochondriac's Dictionary

This weighty tome is illustrated with suitably worrying diagrams to immediately instil in even the healthiest person a mortal fear that they have got at least seven terminal diseases. Includes recently-diagnosed syndromes such as Viagraphobia (fear of having to ask a doctor for anti-impotency pills), Anoraksia Nervosa (whey-faced skeletal appearance, caused by years of obsessively standing on train platforms in a cagoule eating Railtrack sandwiches), Bumbago (lumbar problem resulting from excessive wearing of a heavy bumbag), or Girl Phwooarh Syndrome (experienced by young men immediately after making a lewd comment to a woman in a bar. Symptoms include stabbing pain in the goolies and/or disturbing flashbacks).

101 Dhal Motions
A cautionary tale about the adverse, embarrassing side-effects of consuming too much Indian food.

DIET BOOKS

The Hip and Thigh Diet

How the notorious heavyweight Mike Tyson shed pounds by eating only other peoples' hips and thighs (and the occasional ear).

Food Subtracting for Weight Loss

Sequel to the chart-topping *Food Combining for Weight Loss*, following new medical research suggesting that subtracting is definitely a better idea.

The E-Plan Diet

Forerunner to the F-Plan diet, the (marginally less effective) E-Plan Diet revolves around only consuming foods with an enormous quantity of E-numbers on the label, in the vain hope that resultant chemical-induced hyperactivity will lead to the rapid burning-off of excess calories.

The G-Plan Diet

Successor to the F-Plan Diet, the G-Plan allows dieters to eat whatever they please, but only off items of furniture that they have previously constructed themselves from an Ikea flat-pack. Energy expended via furniture-assembly (and attendant outbursts of violent, physical rage perpetrated with screwdrivers, hammers and an Allen key) will without doubt exceed any calories consumed in the subsequent meal.

The Chip and Pie Diet

Rosemary Conley shows how you can eat unhealthy junk food and still maintain that svelte and lissom figure simply by booking in for thirty grand's worth of liposuction afterwards.

WOMEN

Ex-Lax Nation

Soul-searching social commentary from Elizabeth Pretzel, the self-confessed psychologically fucked-up New Yorker with the laxative abuse habit. 'Full of shite' – *Times Shitty Supplement*.

Frigid Jones' Diary

Thirty-year-old singleton continues to not care in the slightest whether she finds a man or not, since she has gone off the idea of sex entirely and bought a cat instead.

Marital Arts for
Empowered Women

Don't put your personal safety at risk! Marital arts guru Nigel Sprinks, a.k.a 'Squatting Goat', explains how ancient Oriental methods can save you from a life doomed to depressive, cross-stitching singledom. Clear, easy-to-follow diagrams teach even complete beginners the basic arts of Ring Fu (snaring a potential husband), 24-Karate (demanding an expensive, gold engagement band) and Taek Won I-Do (forcing him to vow obedience).

SEX AND EROTICA

The Story of 'Oh ... Was That *It*?'

More first-person descriptions of the female orgasm, which *real* women can actually relate to.

How To Make Love To The Same Person For The Rest of Your Life (Without Your Spouse Finding Out)

The level-headed and practical sequel to the chart-topping *How To Make Love To The Same Person For The Rest of Your Life*.

GARDENING

Gardens Without Brassieres

Charlie 'Ground Force' Dimmock extolls the virtues of urban plant care with unrestrained Bristol Cities. Learn all the tricks of the professional's trade, such as how to use your pendulous swinging nipples as a rudimentary dibber, the best way to convert those redundant 36FF Playtex Cross-Your-Hearts into eye-catching hanging baskets, and which large conifers to plant in order to stop your pervy neighbour leching over your fence whenever you bend over to bed in your nasturtiums.

Women Who Love To Mulch

Self-help for downtrodden, overly-dependent members of the fairer sex who cannot assert themselves sufficiently forcefully to ask their boyfriend to mow the lawn, fork the compost heap or dig the vegetable patch.

Come Into the Garden, Maude

Celebrity horticulture with the ex-Tory frontbencher and former Shadow Health Spokesperson, including useful tips on the permanent removal of common weeds like dandelion, convulvulus, and William Hague.

CLASSICS

The *Aenied* Blyton

Virgil's epic Greek poem, rewritten to appeal to the under-fives. 'Aeneas from Troy was a goodie/But his home got engulfed by a flood. He/Met someone called Dido/And would have said "I do"/Had Dido not died (yuk! How bloody).'

PUZZLES AND QUIZZES

Jeremy Paxman's
Newsnight Quizbook

More testing than the popular *Jeremy Paxman's University Challenge Quizbook,* with questions including: 1. So just what *does* the government plan to do about this current economic crisis? 2. And that's your final response, is it? 3. Oh come *on,* Minister, do you really expect the public to accept that as a coherent policy argument? Answers on page 165.

TEENAGE

Tom Soya

Coming-of-age story set in small-town Islington. Ostracised by schoolmates because of a perceived lactose-intolerance problem which renders him the only kid in class with a lunchbox full of tofu and carob bars, young Tom skips school and, with his young chums from similarly allergy-obsessed middle class households, Cranberry Finn and Non-GM Jim, gets into all manner of scrapes at the local Holland & Barratt store. Printed on 100 per cent recycled, biodegradeable paper from a sustainable forestry plantation.

The *Girls...* Series

Wilhelmina Jackson's refreshingly frank growing-up stories about modern teenage girls continues with four brand new titles: *Girls In Court, Girls In Care, Girls in Therapy* and *Girls Incarcerated In Feltham Young Offenders' Institution*.

BUSINESS AND MANAGEMENT

Eight Habits of Highly Successful People

1. Cocaine.
2. Hookers.
3. Vintage Cristal champagne
4. Going on and on about how much money they've got.
5. Tax evasion.
6. Marrying someone 35 years their junior.
7. Being relentlessly patronising
8. Donating to the Labour Party in exchange for political favours….

How-To-Make-A-Million by Rich T.
Greenbackerstein V, Jnr ('America's
Number One Management Guru')
Rich reveals the trade secrets of how he made his
multimillion-dollar fortune by conning a bunch
of suckers into buying half-assed business
manuals.

GENERAL REFERENCE

The Bumper Book of Fascinating Facts

A book of fascinating facts about vulcanised-rubber vehicular safety devices, such as the fact that the first ever car bumper was patented in 1933 by Messrs Hoffman and Fageol. The ideal Christmas gift for anyone with an interest in automobile impact-absorption systems.

Bridget Jones's Dictionary

Required reading for any pathetic singleton who wants to speak like Helen Fielding's hilarious fictional creation! Compiled in one handy volume, Bridget's entire vocabulary from A to Z: *Aaaaargh!, Alcohol, Arse!, Blokes, Bollocks!, Booze, Boss, Bugger!, Bum (hideously huge), Chardonnay, Cripes!, Darcy, Eeeek!, Fat, Flab, Flobber, Fuck!, Gah!, Good (not v.), HELP!, Hideous (re bum), Huge (re bum)* …

MILITARY FICTION

Sod This For A Game Of Soldiers

The bestselling memoir of a spineless, morally bankrupt deserter who completely avoided playing any part whatsoever in the Gulf War.

Bravo P45

True story of how death-defying SAS soldier Andy McNob survives a helicopter crash, evades his guerrilla captors, dodges hails of bullets, crawls 300 miles across the desert gnawing off his own leg for sustenance, flags down a passing B-52 and returns battered, bruised but heroic to Blighty – only to discover that he has been 'retrenched' in the latest round of defence cutbacks and his wife is shagging some bloke she picked up at the Officers' Club.

NOVELTY AND
GIFT BOOKS

The Little Book of Calm:
Large Print Edition

An entirely average-sized *Book of Calm*.

The Little Book of Undue Alarm

Expounding the philosophy that 'stress breeds success', this book is jam-packed with nuggets of homespun wisdom specially selected to promote doubt, uncertainty and paranoia in an otherwise relaxed individual, thus keeping them alert and on their toes.

National Lottery Numbers *THAT REALLY WORK!*

How do Lottery millionaires do it? This book (written by a bona fide Lottery winner★) reveals the true secrets of those big winners, by *actually printing* sequences of *genuine, proven, guaranteed winning numbers!* Yes, now *YOU* can pick the *very same six balls* that people like Karl Crompton (£10m Jackpot winner) chose. Features over 300 pages of winning sequences (plus Thunderball selections!) including such memorable lines as: 34 02 06 32 17 19, 01 41 35 31 16 09, 09 11 15 16 43 47, 08 12 14 19 24 48 and the (admittedly-controversial) 01 02 03 04 05 06.

[★ Who once scooped £10 on a scratchcard.]

You Don't Know Jack Schott!
by Jack Schott

Foster that gnawing feeling of personal ignorance by dipping into this endlessly intriguing volume, guaranteed to enlighten you as to just how many of the world's most fascinating and essential facts you knew absolutely fuck-all about.

For a current catalogue and a full listing of Summersdale travel books, visit our website:

www.summersdale.com